BOB
HARTMAN's
ASTOUNDING
ALL-AGE
BIBLE
READINGS

for Holidays and Holy Days

kevin
mayhew

**kevin
mayhew**

First published in Great Britain in 2018 by Kevin Mayhew Ltd
Buxhall, Stowmarket, Suffolk IP14 3BW
Tel: +44 (0) 1449 737978 Fax: +44 (0) 1449 737834
E-mail: info@kevinmayhew.com

www.kevinmayhew.com

9 8 7 6 5 4 3 2 1 0

ISBN 978 1 84867 948 1
Catalogue No. 1501577

Cover design by Rob Mortonson
© Images used under licence from Shutterstock Inc.
Typeset by Angela Selfe
Printed and bound in Great Britain

CONTENTS

YEAR C

ABOUT THE AUTHOR

Bob Hartman has been a professional storyteller for 30 years. An ordained minister, he has written over 70 books, for both children and adults, many of them retellings of Bible stories and passages. He is also the author of YouVersion's Bible App for Kids, which has been downloaded over 20 million times. His passion is to help people of every age find their way into the Bible, engage with it, and discover the God who inspired it.

Bob is married to Sue, has two married children, Kari and Chris, and five grandchildren: Malachi, Leah, Jacob, Remy and Sloane.

INTRODUCTION

This book is an invitation.

Come with me, as we enter into these passages from the Bible through action and response. Play along. Reflect. Enjoy.

Come, all ages, as well. The book isn't just for kids. It's not just for grown-ups. It really is meant for everyone. The interactive nature of it is intended to open the scriptures in a way that everyone feels welcome.

Come, because it's simple to use. The instructions are (hopefully!) easy to follow. And the responses are in a different font from the rest of the text, so they are clear and easy to see. The enclosed CD-Rom is there to help you if you need extra text copies or want to project the words on-screen for all the congregation to see.

Come, and follow God's Big Story. The readings are from Years A, B, and C of the Revised Common Lectionary, and they focus on the main holy days of the Christian year. That's because those days, in particular, trace the course of God's Big Story. So even if you belong to a church that doesn't use the Lectionary, this book is still for you, because the readings in this book will help you journey from Creation to Fall to Israel to Incarnation to Passion to Resurrection to Church to Forever.

So come, come and experience God's Word as it has been experienced through the ages: in a group, a gathering, a congregation. Everyone invited. Each encouraged to engage and respond. Come, come and enjoy God's Word. Together.

YEAR A

ADVENT

Matthew 24:36-44

Telling tips:

It might be helpful to use two people to lead this reading. Have one of them do the narration and have the other one lead the group in their actions.

If you want to use one person, then that person will need to explain, at the beginning, that he will be doing a series of actions that the crowd needs to then repeat.

Tear up all your calendars,
switch off all your phones,
throw your fancy timepieces away.
Jesus will be coming back
and no one knows the year,
the hour or the decade or the day.

For the coming of the Son of Man will be just like the days of Noah.

Before the flood came, people were doing ordinary,
everyday things like eating.
Lead everyone in an eating motion.

Before the flood came, people were doing ordinary,
everyday things like drinking.
Lead everyone in a drinking motion.

Before the flood came, people were doing ordinary,
everyday things like getting married.
Have everyone pretend to hold a bunch of flowers and say, 'I do'.

Then Noah went into the ark and the flood came.
And it swept them all away. Without warning. Just like that.
Have everyone throw their arms in the air, wave them about and scream.
And that's exactly how it will be when the Son of Man comes.

Two men will be working in the field.
One will be taken.
Have half the group wave, 'Bye bye!'
One will remain.
Have the other half look around and say, 'Where'd he go?'

Two women will be grinding grain.
One will be taken.
Have half the group wave, 'Bye bye!'
One will remain.
Have the other half look around and say, 'Where'd she go?'

So, stay awake. Be ready. Because you simply don't know when the Lord is coming.

Think about this for a minute.
If the homeowner knew which hour the thief was coming, he'd be awake,
waiting for him, with the cops on speed dial. And then he'd open the door
and simply say, 'You're not breaking in here tonight, mate.'
Have everyone pretend to open door and repeat that line.

In the same way, you have to be prepared and ready.
For the Son of Man is coming when you least expect him.

Tear up all your calendars,
switch off all your phones,
throw your fancy timepieces away.
Jesus will be coming back
and no one knows the year,
the hour or the decade or the day.

CHRISTMAS EVE

Luke 2:(1-7), 8-20

Telling tips:

You will need to recruit a few volunteers for this one. They can either stand with you, at the front, or pop up from where they are sitting (so long as they can be heard). As you will see, you will need volunteers for 1) reading the emperor's decree (you might like to provide them with a scroll), 2) Mary and Joseph, 3) the angel.

As for the crowd actions, simply warn them that there will be actions throughout the reading, and that you will tell them what to do, show them, and then do it with them. You can use a second person to do this, instead.

The Emperor wanted to count up all his people
so, everyone went to their home town.
Walking motion.

So, Joseph took Mary to the place that he was from.
Bethlehem, a long way down.
Hand over eye, look into distance.

The story begins with a decree.
A volunteer reads: 'Hear ye, hear ye! By order of the Roman Emperor Augustus, everyone must return to their home town to be counted.'

So, everyone, everywhere, in the Roman Empire took their families to the place from which they originally came.
Have everyone in the building get up and move, in family groups, to different seats.

Joseph was descended from King David's family, so he and Mary, to whom he was engaged, travelled from Nazareth in Galilee, 90 miles south, to Bethlehem, the city of David. Mary was expecting a baby.
As this is read, volunteers playing Joseph and Mary walk slowly from the back of the room and take a seat at the front.

While they were staying in Bethlehem, the time came for Mary to give birth to her baby. The upstairs room, where the rest of the family stayed, was full.

Have everyone jostle their neighbour and shout, 'No room!' And while they are doing this, have Mary produce a baby and sit and hold it.

So, Mary gave birth to her firstborn son in the downstairs room, where the animals were kept.

Have everyone 'moo'.

Then she wrapped her baby in strips of cloth and laid him in the feed trough.

Have everyone go 'Awwww'.

In that area, there were shepherds, out in the fields, watching their sheep at night.

Have everyone make a peeping motion and then go 'baa'.

Suddenly, one of God's angels appeared to the shepherds. God's glory shone all around them. And they were terrified.

Have everyone scream.

But the angel said to them:
A volunteer reads: Don't be afraid. I have good news, sure to bring you joy. In the city of David, your Saviour is born. Christ the Lord.
And here's the sign that what I say is true:
you will find the child, wrapped in strips of cloth. And lying in a manger.

And when the angel had finished, a crowd of angels joined him, saying:

Everyone says: 'Glory to God on high! And peace to all his people!'

When the angels left, the shepherds hurried to Bethlehem.

Have everyone leave their seats again and move to other seats.

They told Mary and Joseph and the rest of the family about the angels and what the angels had said.

Everyone shouts, 'It was amazing!'

And Mary kept it all, like a treasure, in her heart.

Mary puts hand on heart.

Then the shepherds went back to their sheep, praising God for what they had heard and seen.

Everyone shouts again, 'Glory to God on high! And peace to all his people!'

CHRISTMAS DAY

Hebrews 1:1-12

Telling tips:
Divide your group into two groups, one side for the Angels, the other side for Jesus. Teach each group its line ahead of time. Then just have each group shout out their line when you point in their direction.

In the past, God talked to our ancestors in all sorts of different ways through the prophets. (As an option, it could be fun to have everyone in the room shout out names of Old Testament prophets.)

But these days, things are different, for now God has spoken to us through his Son.
Jesus side shouts 'That's Jesus!'

(The Narrator might want to start small here, and then build with each passing reference to the nature of Jesus.)

His Son, who inherited everything from him.
Jesus side shouts 'That's Jesus!'

His Son, through whom he made the world.
Jesus side shouts 'That's Jesus!'

His Son, who reflects God's glory.
Jesus side shouts 'That's Jesus!'

His Son, who is the very image of God, himself.
Jesus side shouts 'That's Jesus!'

His Son, whose mighty word sustains the world.
Jesus side shouts 'That's Jesus!'

His Son, who purified us from our sins.
Jesus side shouts 'That's Jesus!'

His Son, who then sat down at God's right-hand side on high.
Jesus side shouts 'That's Jesus!'

His Son, who stands even above the angels.
Jesus side shouts 'That's Jesus!'

Did God ever say to the angels, 'You are my son, today I have begotten you.'?
Angel side shake heads and say, 'Nope'.

Did God ever say to the angels, 'I will be his Father. He will be my son.'?
Angel side shake heads and say, 'Nope'.

And did God ever say to the angels, 'Let all God's angels worship him' – the very thing he said when his firstborn son came into the world?
Angel side shake heads and say, 'Nope'.

Can you spot the difference?

This is what God says about the angels:

'He makes his angels wind and fiery flames.'

But this is what God says about his Son:

'Your throne, O God, lasts forever. And righteousness is the sceptre with which you reign.'
Jesus side shouts 'That's Jesus!'

'You love what's good. You hate what's evil. So God, your God, has blessed you more than any other.'
Jesus side shouts 'That's Jesus!'

'In the beginning, you made the earth. The heavens were made by your hands.'
Jesus side shouts 'That's Jesus!'

'And while heaven and earth will wear out, like a faded pair of jeans, you will last forever.'
Jesus side shouts 'That's Jesus!'

'Heaven and earth? You'll roll them up like a cloak. You'll change them like a set of clothes. But you will stay the same. Forever!'
Jesus side shouts 'That's Jesus!'

EPIPHANY

Matthew 2:1-12

Telling tips:

Divide your group into three groups. One for Herod. One for the Wise Men. And one for the Chief Priests and Scribes. Teach them their lines, as below.

During the reign of King Herod

Herod group rub hands together and say, 'I'm the Bad Guy'.

and after Jesus was born in Bethlehem, certain visitors came to Jerusalem: Wise men from the east.

Wise Men group sing just the first six words of 'We three kings of Orient are' and then say: 'We're the Good Guys'.

Round the city the Wise Men went.

Wise Men action

Asking one question and one question only.

Have the Wise Men group repeat the following, line by line, after you.

'A child has been born. Born King of the Jews. We saw his star in the sky. Please tell us where he is. We want to honour him.'

King Herod

Herod action

was frightened by this news. And all Jerusalem trembled with him.

So, he gathered all the chief priests and scribes.

Chief Priest and Scribe group hold Bibles in the air and say, 'We know the scriptures. We know them well.'

And he asked them where the Messiah was supposed to be born.

And the chief priests and scribes

Chief Priests and Scribes action

said to him:

Have the Chief Priests and Scribe group repeat the lines after you.

'Bethlehem, in Judea. That's what the prophets say.'

So, Herod

Herod action

arranged a secret meeting with the wise men.

Wise Men action

And asked them to tell him precisely when they had seen the star.

And when they told him, he sent them to Bethlehem. And here is what he said:

Have the Herod group repeat this line by line after you.

'Search for the child. And when you have found him, tell me where he is.

So I can honour him, too.'

So, off the Wise Men went,

Wise Men action

following the star. And when it stopped above the place where the child was,
they were overcome with joy.

They went into the house. There was the child and Mary, his mother. They knelt down
before him. They honoured him. Then, from their treasure chests, they drew out:

Have the Wise Men group say, after you:

Gold,
Frankincense
and Myrrh.

That night the Wise Men

Wise Men action

had a dream warning them not to return to Herod.

Herod action

So, they went home by another route completely.

TRANSFIGURATION

Matthew 17:1-9

Telling tips:

There is effectively an action at the end of every line in this reading. Warn your group about this and then tell them to repeat whatever you do. You can also use a second reader to lead the group. This one, as you will see, is probably best done standing and in a shouty manner.

Six days passed. And then Jesus said, 'C'mon Peter!'
Tell everyone to shout, 'C'mon Peter!'

And then Jesus said, 'C'mon, James!'
Tell everyone to shout, 'C'mon, James!'

And then Jesus said, 'C'mon, John!'
Tell everyone to shout, 'C'mon, John!'

And he led them up a mountain.
Tell everyone to walk. Then stop. Then huff and puff.

When they reached the top, right there, in front of them, Jesus was transfigured.
Tell everyone to shout, 'Transfigured? Go figure!'

His face shone like the sun.
Tell everyone to shout, 'We're stunned!'

And his clothes turned white as light.
Tell everyone to shout, 'That's bright!'

Then, out of nowhere, Moses appeared.
Tell everyone to shout, 'Pharaoh, let my people go!'

And Elijah showed up, too.

Tell everyone to shout, 'Idol worship's a no-no!'

The prophets talked with Jesus, and then Peter said:

Tell everyone to shout, 'It's good we're here. Let's build a tent for each of you!'

But as Peter spoke, a bright cloud passed over them and a voice from the cloud said:

Tell everyone to shout, 'THIS is my beloved Son, with whom I am very pleased. Listen to HIM!'

When they heard what the voice said, the disciples buried their faces in the ground, terrified.

Tell everyone to hide their face and shout, 'AAAAAAHHHHHH!'

But Jesus touched them and said:

Tell everyone to whisper gently, 'Get up. Don't be afraid.'

And when they looked up, Moses and Elijah were gone. Only Jesus remained.

Tell everyone to give a relieved sigh.

So Jesus led them back down the mountain.

Tell everyone to walk. Then stop. Then huff and puff.

And as they went, he said:

Tell everyone to say, 'Don't tell anyone what you saw today until the Son of Man is raised from the dead.'

ASH WEDNESDAY

Matthew 6:1-6, 16-21

Telling tips:
This is another reading where you show the group the actions as you go along. Again, if you want, you can use a second person to lead the group.

Watch out. If you do good and religious things just to impress other people, you won't impress your Father in heaven. You won't score any brownie points with him.

So, when you give money to the poor, don't blow a trumpet to shout: 'Hey, look at me. See how good I am!'
Have everyone shout: 'Hey look at me. See how good I am!'
That's what hypocrites do, just so other people will admire them. And that, and that alone, will be their reward.

Look at your left hand.
Have everyone look at their left hand.
Now look at your right hand.
Have everyone do that, too.
When you give money to the poor, don't even let your left hand know what your right hand is doing.

That way, what you give to the poor will be a lovely secret
have everyone say 'shhhh!'
between you and God. And the One who sees every secret will reward you.

And when you pray, don't stand on the street corners or the synagogues to shout: 'Hey, look at me. See how good I am!'
Have everyone shout: 'Hey, look at me. See how good I am!', in a faux holy voice.
That's what hypocrites do, just so other people will admire them. And that, and that alone, will be their reward.

Instead, when you pray, go into your room and shut the door behind you.
Have everyone make a shutting door motion — with a squeak, if you like.
That way, your prayers will be a lovely secret

Have everyone say 'shhhh!'
between you and God. And the One who sees every secret will reward you.

And when you fast, don't walk around looking miserable.
Don't look all hollow-eyed and hungry and say:
'Hey, look at me. See how good I am.'
Have everyone say: 'Hey, look at me. See how good I am!'
in a weak and croaky fashion.
That's what hypocrites do, just so other people will admire them. And that, and that alone, will be their reward.

Instead, when you fast, do what you can to look as happy and healthy as possible.
Have everyone point to face and smile.
That way, your fast will be a lovely secret
have everyone say 'shhhh!'
between you and God. And the One who sees every secret will reward you.

Earth's not the place to store up treasure.
Moths are everywhere. And rust. And thieves. They'll soon take everything you have.

Store your treasure in heaven, instead, where moths don't chew and rust doesn't break through and thieves have no thieving to do.

For where your treasure is, that's where your heart will call home.

PALM SUNDAY

Matthew 21:1-11

Telling tips:
Most of the actions/responses come at the start of each section. You can lead them in that, yourself, or have a second person do it.

It was like a secret mission.
Have everyone whisper 'SHHHHHH'.

Jesus and his disciples were at the Mount of Olives, outside of Bethpage, near Jerusalem. 'Go into the village,' said Jesus to his disciples. 'You'll find a donkey there, tied up with her colt. Bring them to me. And if anyone should ask you what you're doing, just say "The Lord needs them." That's the password. And they'll let you go on your way.'

It was like a surprise.
Have everyone shout 'Surprise!'

Kings ride on stallions. But the prophet Zechariah said that, one day,
God's people would get a humble king, a king who rode on a donkey.

So, the disciples did what Jesus told them. They fetched the donkey and the colt, put their cloaks on them, and Jesus hopped on for a ride.

It was like a parade.
Have everyone stand up and march and while they are marching, say the following:

A great crowd gathered. Some laid their cloaks on the ground. Others cut branches from trees and laid them on the ground, too. And they all shouted the very thing you'd shout to a king.
Have everyone shout this after you, line by line.

'Hosanna to David's Son!'
'Blessed is the One who comes in the Lord's name!'
'Hosanna in heaven on high!'

It was like a puzzle.
Have everyone scratch their head and go 'Huh?'

When the parade entered Jerusalem, the citizens were confused. 'Who is this?' they asked.

And the crowd that followed the king on the donkey simply said:
Have everyone shout this, too.

'It's Jesus, who comes from Nazareth!'
'It's Jesus, the prophet from Galilee!'

YEAR A

GOOD FRIDAY

John 18:1–19:42

Telling tips:
My hope is that the actions can be done sitting down and quietly to reflect the nature of the reading and the day. The scripture passages you need to read are listed between the responses, so use whichever translation you prefer.
I think this reading would work better if done by two leaders, one to read the passage and one to lead the crowd and demonstrate the actions.

Come into the garden, with Jesus and his disciples.
Hold a beautiful flower in your hands.

Read 18:1

Now join the guards and soldiers, arriving there with Judas.
Hold your torch or lantern high.

Read 18:2-9

Now grab your sword like Peter.
Strike off the servant's ear.

Read 18:10-14

Now point your finger in an accusing manner.

Read 18:15-18

Now pretend to strike someone across the face.

Read 18:19-24

Now hold your hands in front of you, as if warming them at a fire.

Read 18:25-27

Now cross your wrists, as if bound, in front of you.

Read 18:28-40

Now place a crown on your head and hold it there.

Read 18:35–19:5

Now make an angry face and shake your fist.

Read 19:6-15

Now hunch over and pretend to hold a heavy cross beam.

Read 19:16-22

Now pretend to throw dice.

Read 19:23-25

Put your hand to your throat as if thirsty.

Read 19:26-29

Lower your head and close your eyes.

Read 19:30-37

Now pretend to carry someone in your arms.

Read 19:38-42

EASTER DAY

John 20:1-18

Telling tips:

This is meant to be a companion to the Good Friday reading. So, it will work in the same way – an action followed by a reading. But to reflect the difference between the days and the movement in the passage, this one will be very 'up' and active. Oh, and you will need to divide your group into two groups for the Peter and John section.

Once again, the scripture passages you need to read are listed between the responses, so use whichever translation you prefer.

Everyone stand up.

Read John 20:1

Now everyone run in their place, then stop and catch breath.

Read 20:2

Now everyone run again but tell the 'John' side to run faster.

Read 20:3-4

Everyone bend over, as if looking into something low.

Read 20:5-11

Now everyone sit down and draw a halo round your head.

Read 20:12-13

Now everyone stand again, with arms forward.

Read 20:14-17

Now everyone run again.

Read 20:18

ASCENSION

Luke 24:44-53

Telling tips:
A simple set of motions to introduce each part of the passage. You might want to practise them with the crowd before you begin the reading.

'Look back!' said Jesus (more or less) to his disciples.
Everybody look back!

'Back to the law of Moses and the prophets and the psalms. They pointed to me. And what they said was fulfilled in me.'

Then he helped them to understand those scriptures.

'Now, look to yourselves!'
Everybody look at their neighbour.

'Those scriptures clearly say that the Messiah was supposed to suffer, then rise again on the third day. So witnesses, like you, who have seen it all, must go and tell every nation that they need to repent and that they can find forgiveness in the Messiah's name. Every nation, starting right here, in Jerusalem.'

'Now, look ahead.'
Everyone look ahead.

'I am going to send you what the Father promised. So, I want you to stay here, in Jerusalem, till that promise comes – till you have been clothed with God's power.'

Finally, look up.
Everyone look up.

Then Jesus led them to Bethany, where he lifted his hands and blessed them. And while he was doing that, Jesus himself was lifted up – lifted up to heaven – as they watched.

Then they worshipped Jesus and, filled with joy, returned to Jerusalem and praised God in the Temple.

PENTECOST

Acts 2:1-21

Telling tips:
Divide your congregation into two groups. One for the followers of Jesus, the other for the crowd gathered in Jerusalem. Lead them, in turn, in the following actions. And have a bit of fun!

On the day of Pentecost, the followers of Jesus were gathered together in one place. A sound, like a wild wind, came from heaven and blew through that place.

Have followers group make a blowy, rushing wind sound.

Then tongues of fire rested on each of their heads.

Have followers group point to each other's heads and shout 'Fire!' or give an amazed gasp.

And with that, they were filled with God's Holy Spirit and started talking in languages they did not know. All through the Spirit's power.

If you think it's appropriate, have the followers group speak out phrases in whatever foreign language they know. Encourage them to get louder and louder and louder.

Because of the feast of Pentecost, Jews from all over the world were gathered in Jerusalem. When they heard the followers of Jesus speaking in each of their native tongues, they were confused.

Have crowd group turn to each other and give a bewildered shrug.

And they said to each other:

Have the crowd group repeat each of these lines after you. Have a bit of fun with the fact that the lines go on and on, and also with the different country names. You might want to take a deep breath in the middle of the list.

'Aren't these people just Galilean?'
'How is that they know each of our languages?'
'We're Parthians, Medes and Elamites.'

'We come from Mesopotamia, Judea, and Cappadocia.'
'From Pontus and Asia.'
'From Phrygia and Pamphilia.'
'From Egypt and that Cyrenian bit of Libya.'
'From Rome, both Jews and converts to Judaism.'
'Cretans and Arabs, too.'
'Yet we hear them speak about God's great deeds in our own languages.'

So together they cried:
Have them shout this.

'What does this mean?'

There were some, however, who sneered and said:
Make this a surprise. Use your band members maybe, or a couple of servers, or your ministers. Tell them their line ahead of time, and their cue.

'Nah, they're just drunk.'

So, Peter stood up and answered the crowd's question.

'We're not drunk,' he said. 'It's only nine in the morning. No, this is what the prophet Joel said would happen.

"In the last days," says God, "I will pour out my spirit on everyone. Your sons and daughters will prophesy. Your young men will see visions and your old men will dream dreams. Even on slaves, both men and women, I will pour out my spirit, and they too will prophesy.

There will be warning signs in the sky and signs on the earth, as well.
Blood and fire and smoke. The sun will turn black, the moon red as blood, before God's Big Day arrives. Then everyone who calls on God's name will be saved."'

TRINITY

Psalm 8

Telling tips:
The scripture passages you need to read are listed between the responses, so use whichever translation you prefer.

Have everyone stand and lift their hands in the air.

Read 8:1

Have everyone pretend to cradle a baby in their arms and look down at her.

Read 8:2

Have everyone pretend to extend a telescope and look through it up into the sky. As an alternative, have everyone wiggle their fingers.

Read 8:3

Have everyone look at their neighbour(s).

Read 8:4

Have everyone set a pretend crown on the head of one neighbour.

Read 8:5

Have everyone look at their feet.

Read 8:6

Have everyone baa or moo.

Read 8:7

Have everyone flap wings or make a fish face.

Read 8:8

Have everyone repeat the first, hands in air, position.

Read 8:9

HARVEST

Deuteronomy 8:7-18

Telling tips:
The scripture passages you need to read are listed between the responses, so use whichever translation you prefer.

Read 8:7

With hands outstretched or lifted up, all say: 'We Praise you for Providing, Lord.'

Read 8:8

With hands outstretched or lifted up, all say: 'We Praise you for Providing, Lord.'

Read 8:9

With hands outstretched or lifted up, all say: 'We Praise you for Providing, Lord.'

Read 8:10

With hands outstretched or lifted up, all say: 'We Praise you for Providing, Lord.'

(At this point, you might want to have folks think about what specific aspect of God's provision they are thankful for, and then speak those out, share and pray in small groups, illustrate and put up on a wall or board at the front. Then finish with the response:)

With hands outstretched or lifted up, all say: 'We Praise you for Providing, Lord.'

Read 8:11

With heads bowed, all say: 'Forgive us for Forgetting, Lord.'

Read 8:12-14

With heads bowed, all say: 'Forgive us for Forgetting, Lord.'

Read 8:15-17

With heads bowed, all say: 'Forgive us for Forgetting, Lord.'

(Perhaps a time of prayer here, where folks call to mind the time they have forgotten God's provision, through their pride and disobedience. Then finish with the response:)

With heads bowed, all say: 'Forgive us for Forgetting, Lord.'

Then, lead all to put hands on heart and head and say:
'Remind us to Remember, Lord.'

Read 8:18

Then finish with the three responses:

We Praise you for Providing, Lord.
Forgive us our Forgetting, Lord.
Remind us to Remember, Lord.
Amen.

ALL SAINTS

Revelation 7:9-17

Telling tips:
Divide your crowd in two. One group in the middle, surrounded by the second group. Tell the first group to stand and pretend to wave palm branches while you talk.

So, I looked and what I saw was a multitude of people, a crowd too big to count. And, in that crowd, there were people from every nation and tribe and tongue. They stood in front of the throne, they stood before the Lamb. They wore white robes and there were palm branches in their hands. And here is what they shouted, shouted loud and strong:

Have them shout this after you:

'Salvation belongs to our God. To our God who is seated on the throne.
To our God and to the Lamb.'

Now tell the second group to stand.

Then say: All of the angels stood around the throne. And around the elders, too.
And the four living creatures.

Then the angels fell on their faces, in front of the throne. And they worshipped God.

Tell the second group to sit down, bow down, whatever is appropriate, and then say after you:

'This is what our God deserves. Blessing and Glory. Wisdom and thanksgiving.
Honour and power and might. Forever and ever. Amen!'

Then one of the elders said to me, 'Who are these people wearing white robes?
Where have they come from?'
'Sir,' I said. 'You know, surely?'
'They are the ones who have come through the great tribulation,' he said.

'They washed their robes in the blood of the Lamb and made them white. And that is why they are here before the throne of God. They worship him, all day long and all night, too, in his temple. And God will protect them. They will no longer be hungry or thirsty or be burned by the scorching sun. For the Lamb will be their shepherd. He will guide them to the water of life. And God will wipe away their tears.'

YEAR B

ADVENT

Isaiah 64:1-9

Telling tips:
The scripture passages you need to read are listed between the responses, so use whichever translation you prefer.

Read 64:1

Action: pretend to tear a sheet of paper in half, from top to bottom.

Read 64:2

Action: make a bubbling sound.

Read 64:3

Action: quiver and shake.

Read 64:4

Action: point one finger to ear, another to eye.

Read 64:5

Action: hide face with hands.

Read 64:6

Action: pretend to hold leaf in hands, then blow it away.

Read 64:7

Action: repeat hiding motion.

Read 64:8

Action: pretend to shape pot with hands.

Read 64:9

Action: hide face and then remove hands and stretch out arms.

CHRISTMAS EVE

Isaiah 9:2-7

Telling tips:

Tell the crowd what to do, along the way. Something like, 'In the next verse, when you hear x, do y.' Again, you could use two readers and have the second reader give the instructions and lead the crowd. The scripture passages you need to read are listed between the responses, so use whichever translation you prefer.

Read 9:2

When you say 'darkness', have everyone shut their eyes, and cover their eyes with their hands. Then, when you say 'light' have them take their hands away and open their eyes. You can either do it in the first line, or in both.

Read 9:3

When you mention 'Harvest', have everyone turn to a neighbour, pretend to hold a large vegetable in their hands and say: 'Is this not a magnificent marrow?'

Read 9:4

When you say 'yoke' or 'bar across the shoulders' have everyone pretend they are carrying a heavy yoke on their shoulders. Then when you mention that the yoke is broken, have them pretend to throw it off.

Read 9:5

When you say, 'tramping warriors', have everyone stamp their feet. When you burn the garments in the fire, have everyone throw their hands forward with a whoosh!

Read 9:6

Have everyone reach out their hands as if placing them on a young man's shoulders. Then have them repeat his four names after you.

Read 9:7

Have everyone lift up their arms with a big 'Hooray!'

CHRISTMAS DAY

John 1:1-14

Telling tips:

Divide your group into three.

The first group is 'The Word'.
When you point to them, they point to their mouths and shout 'The Word!'
The second group is 'John'.
When you point to them, they pretend to dunk someone and shout 'John!'
The third group is 'The Light'.
When you point to them, they pretend to flick a light switch or pull the string to light a bulb above and shout 'The Light!'

THE WORD was in the beginning.

THE WORD was with God.

THE WORD was God.

THE WORD was in the beginning with God.

THE WORD made everything. Absolutely everything.

Life was in THE WORD.

And that life was THE LIGHT for everyone. Absolutely everyone.

THE LIGHT shines in the dark. And the dark did not destroy it.

JOHN was a man who was sent by God.

JOHN was sent as a witness to THE LIGHT. To point people to THE LIGHT.
So that everyone might be drawn to THE LIGHT.

But JOHN was not THE LIGHT. JOHN simply came to show the way.

For THE LIGHT, the true light that brings light to everyone, was coming into the world.

THE LIGHT was in the world. THE LIGHT made the world.
But the world did not know who he was.

THE LIGHT came to his own people and even they did not accept him.

But those who received THE LIGHT, and those who believed THE LIGHT,
were given power to become God's children.

That's right, children, not born naturally, in a flesh and blood way,
but brought to life by God himself.

So, THE WORD became human. THE WORD lived among us.
And we have seen how glorious he is. Glorious as only the Father's son can be.
THE WORD, full of grace and truth.

EPIPHANY

Isaiah 60:1-6

Telling tips:

You will need one person (or a very small group of people) to stand at the front and represent Israel. They will need to begin seated, or kneeling.

Divide the rest of your group into four groups:

- Nurses carrying babies
- Sea creatures (fish, octopi, sharks, whatever)
- People carrying big bags of money (in arms, on their shoulders)
- Camels (walk in a bouncy way, with an occasional spit)

60:1

(To the group at the front) Stand up! Shine!

Have them hold their hands in the air. Either demonstrate this for them at the time or tell them about it beforehand.

For your light has arrived and God's glory has risen upon you.

60:2

As for the rest of the earth and its people, they are covered in darkness.

Have everyone apart from those at the front put their hands over their faces.

But God's Glory will shine on you!

60:3

And that is why the rest of the world will be drawn to your light.

Why kings will bask in the brightness of your dawn.

Have everyone apart from the group at the front remove their hands from their faces, look at the group at the front, reach their arms out to them and say 'Wow!'

60:4

To the group at the front say: Look, look around.
Have them look around.
Do you see? They're gathering. They're coming.
Sons from far away. Daughters in their nurses' arms.
This group does its action while making its way to the front.

60:5

And when you see this, you will shine even more brightly. You will be thrilled.
You will rejoice. For the abundance of the seas will come to you.
Sea creature group comes forward with actions.
And the wealth of the nations, too.
People carrying money bags come forward.

60:6

You will be overwhelmed with camels.
Camels come forward.
Young camels from Midian and Ephah. And on their backs will be the people of Sheba,
bearing gold and frankincense and singing the praises of God.

And then, with everyone gathered at the front and in the aisles, you might want
to sing the praises of God together, too.

TRANSFIGURATION

2 Kings 2:1-12

Telling tips:
Divide your group into three groups, one for Elijah, one for Elisha, and one for the company of the prophets. It will work best if the prophet group is next to the Elisha group. Tell each group that they are to repeat the lines of their characters and the actions, after you have said the lines.

2:1

When the time had come for God to take Elijah to heaven in a whirlwind, Elijah and Elisha were in Gilgal.

2:2

So, Elijah said to Elisha:
Have Elijah group point to the ground and repeat the following line.
'Stay here. The Lord wants me to carry on to Bethel.'

But Elisha said to Elijah:
Have the Elisha group shake their heads and repeat the following line.
'As God lives and you live, I will not leave you!'

So, together they went to Bethel.

2:3

When they got to Bethel, a bunch of prophets came to Elisha and said:
Have the prophet group put their hand to the side of their mouth as if whispering, lean in the direction of the Elisha group and then repeat the following line, in a loud whisper.
'Do you know that God will take your master away today?'

And Elisha whispered back:

Have Elisha group do whispering motion and repeat the following line, in the direction of the prophet group.

'I do! Don't mention it!' (They could also say, 'Keep quiet!' or 'Keep shtum!')

2:4

Then Elijah said to Elisha:

Have Elijah group point to the ground and repeat the following line.

'Stay here. The Lord wants me to carry on to Jericho.'

But Elisha said to Elijah:

Have the Elisha group shake their heads and repeat the following line.

'As God lives and you live, I will not leave you.'

So, together they went to Jericho.

2:5

When they got to Jericho, a bunch of prophets came to Elisha and said:

Have the prophet group put their hand to the side of their mouth as if whispering, lean in the direction of the Elisha group and then repeat the following line, in a loud whisper.

'Do you know that God will take your master away today?'

And Elisha whispered back:

Have Elisha group do whispering motion and repeat the following line, in the direction of the prophet group.

'I do! Don't mention it!' (They could also say, 'Keep quiet!' or 'Keep shtum!')

2:6

Then Elijah said to Elisha:

Have Elijah group point to the ground and repeat the following line.

'Stay here. The Lord wants me to carry on to the Jordan river.'

But Elisha said to Elijah:

Have the Elisha group shake their heads and repeat the following line.

'As God lives and you live, I will not leave you.'

So, together they went to the Jordan river.

2:7

Fifty prophets went with them but stood apart from Elijah and Elisha
when they finally reached the river.

2:8

Then Elijah rolled up his cloak and struck the water with it. And when he did,
the river parted so that he and Elisha could cross on dry ground.

2:9

And then, on the far side of the river, Elijah asked Elisha a question.
*Have Elijah group hold out their hands to Elisha group and repeat
the following line.*
'Before I go, what can I do for you?'

And Elisha replied:
*Have Elisha group hold out their hands then pull them back as if receiving
a gift from Elijah group.*
'Give me a double portion of your spirit!'

2:10

And Elijah said:
Have Elisha group repeat the following, line by line.
'That's a tough one!'
'But if you see me as I'm taken, it's yours!'

2:11

So off they went. And as they walked, a chariot of fire drawn by horses of fire
came between them and Elijah went in a whirlwind up to heaven!
(And, yeah, you can have them all hum the 'Chariots of Fire' song as you say this,
if you don't think it's too cheesy!)

2:12

Elisha saw it all. And as Elijah went, he cried:

Have Elisha group reach their hands to heaven and shout.

'Father! Father! It's Israel's chariots and horsemen!'

And when Elijah at last disappeared from view,
Elisha took hold of his clothes and tore them in two.

ASH WEDNESDAY

Psalm 51:1-17

Telling tips:

The scripture passages you need to read are listed between the responses, so use whichever translation you prefer. The reading ties the actions, in a quiet way, to the specific supplications in the Psalm.

So, have everyone bow their heads and hold out their hands as if expecting a gift. Tell them to hold that position as you read and until you tell them to take a new position.

Then read 51:1.

Next, tell them to gently rub their hands along their arms, as if washing themselves.

Then read 51:2-7.

Next, have them hold their hands to their ears and smile, as if hearing good news.

Then read 51:8-9.

Next, have them put their hand on their heart.

Then read 51:10-13.

Finally, have them open their mouths, or put a finger to their lips.

Then read 51:14-17.

BOB
HARTMAN'S
ASTOUNDING
ALL-AGE
BIBLE
READINGS
for Holidays and Holy Days

PALM SUNDAY

John 12:12-16

Telling tips:
Once again, you can use two readers for this, one to read the text and the other to lead the crowd.

A great crowd was in Jerusalem for the Passover Festival.
Have everyone raise their arms and cheer and shout:
'We're a great crowd! A really great crowd!'

Word spread that Jesus was coming to Jerusalem.
Have everyone whisper to their neighbour: 'Jesus is coming to Jerusalem!'

So, the crowd took palm tree branches and went to meet Jesus.
Have everyone wave pretend branches, or real ones, if you have them.

And this is what they shouted.
Have everyone shout the lines after you, line by line.
'Hosanna!'
'Blessed is the one who comes in the Lord's name!'
'Blessed is the King of Israel!'

Jesus sat on a young donkey he'd found.
Have everyone put hands as ears to the sides of their head,
waggle them and go 'hee-haw!'

Why? Because this is what the prophet Zechariah said:
'Don't be frightened, Daughter of Zion. Your king is coming on the colt of a donkey.'
Have everyone repeat the donkey action.

When this happened, Jesus' disciples did not understand what was going on.
Have everyone scratch their head and go: 'Huh! Don't get it.'

But after Jesus was crucified and raised from the dead and ascended to heaven, they remembered what had happened and the prophecies about him and understood it all.
Have everyone point their finger in the air and smile and say,
'We get it, now, we really do!'

GOOD FRIDAY

Isaiah 52:13 – 53:12

Telling tips:

Unlike some of the other pieces, this one will work best if the words are either projected or printed on a service order. Rather than a response, the crowd lines are meant to lead the reading and unpack it.

All: Tell us about your servant.

Reader: He will prosper, lifted up to the highest place.

All: But look at him. How is that possible?

Reader: True, his appearance is startling. Marred, disfigured, hardly human. But startling and surprising is what he is all about. He will astonish the nations and shut the mouths of kings. For he will show them something they could never have imagined.

All: It seems kind of hard to believe.

Reader: What can I say? It's what God himself has shown us.

All: But, like a dried-up plant, there was nothing attractive about him. Nothing to draw us to him. He was rejected, despised. Suffering, ill. A man no one wanted to look at. A man no one valued.

Reader: True, we looked at him and thought that God had caused his suffering and his illness. But the truth is that it was our illness he bore, our disease he took upon himself. He was wounded for our sins, crushed for the evil we had done. And by his punishment we are healed. By his wounds we are made whole.

All: We are sinners, that's true. Like sheep, we have all wandered away. We have all insisted on doing our own thing. On living My Way.

Reader: And God has put our sin on his shoulders. He was bruised and he was beaten. But, like a lamb led to slaughter or a sheep before its shearer, he didn't say a thing.

All: He takes our punishment? But how is that right?

Reader: His death was a perversion of justice, that's true. Who could see, at the time, that there would be any positive outcome from that? But there was. He died for the sins of God's people.

All: But he was innocent, right? Buried with the wicked in a rich man's tomb, even though he'd never told a lie or hurt anyone?

Reader: True. All true. But that was God's decision. All the pain he suffered. He was an offering for sin. And, as a result, he received God's reward: he will see his 'children'. His days will be long. And God's will shall be done through him.

All: So, light will come from pain. And he will know it and be satisfied. The righteous one will bear the sins of the unrighteousness and make them righteous, too.

Reader: And he will take his place alongside the great ones. For, in death he stood with us, with sinners. That he might take our sin upon himself and take that sin away.

EASTER DAY

Mark 16:1-8

Telling tips:

It's probably best to use a couple of readers. One to read the text and the other to lead the crowd. The scripture passages you need to read are listed between the responses, so use whichever translation you prefer.

Read 16:1

Have everyone pretend to hold a packet/bundle/bottle of spice in their hands.

Read 16:2-3

Have everyone whisper to their neighbour: 'Who will roll away the stone for us from the entrance to the tomb?'

Read 16:4

Have everyone pretend to roll the stone away.

Read 16:5

Have everyone scream.

Read 16:6

Have everyone gesture with their hands, as if pointing out the place where Jesus had been.

Read 16:7

Have everyone point and say: 'Go!'

Read 16:8

At the word 'terror', have everyone scream again. At the word 'amazement', have everyone shout: 'Wow!'

ASCENSION

Psalm 93

Telling tips:
With each call and response, get louder and louder. It might be best to project this one or print it on an order of service.

Verse One:

Reader: The Lord is King.

All: He's robed in majesty.

Reader: The Lord is King.

All: He's robed in majesty.

Reader: The Lord is King.

All: He's robed in majesty.

Reader: He made the world, immovable.

Verse Two:

Reader: His throne is old.

All: He's everlasting.

Reader: His throne is old.

All: He's everlasting.

Reader: His throne is old.

All: He's everlasting.

Reader: He's established it forever.

Verse Three:

Reader: The floods arise.

    All: Their roar majestic.

Reader: The floods arise.

    All: Their roar majestic.

Reader: The floods arise.

    All: Their roar majestic.

Reader: But God is more majestic still.

(You might want to do this last verse the opposite way, so it gets more and more quiet and reverent.)

Verse Four:

Reader: His laws are sure.

    All: His house is holy.

Reader: His laws are sure.

    All: His house is holy.

Reader: His laws are sure.

    All: His house is holy.

Reader: He is Lord forevermore.

PENTECOST

Ezekiel 37:1-14

Telling tips:

Have everyone stand, if they are able, and shut their eyes. The responses are meant to help the crowd meditate and reflect on the passage they have just heard. It would be helpful to have one person read the scripture passage and another person read the meditation. The scripture passages you need to read are listed between the responses, so use whichever translation you prefer.

Read 37:1

Say, 'Bones. Can you see the bones? Femurs and fibulas. Spines and skulls. Rib cages wrecked and scattered. Bones. Can you see the bones?'

Read 37:2

Then say, 'Dust. Can you taste the dust? Ancient and desiccated. Cloudy, consuming. Rising and choking. Dry as death. Dust. Can you taste the dust?'

Read 37:3

Then say, 'Words. Can you hear the words? God's words. Impossible words. Word of wonder. Words of hope. Words. Can you hear the words?'

Read 37:4-7

Then say, 'Rattling. Can you hear the rattling? Bone against bone. Clattering, colliding. Skeletons rising. Rising from the dust of death. Rattling. Can you hear the rattling?'

Read 37:8

Then say, 'Flesh. Can you see the flesh? Muscles and blood vessels. Organs and nerves. Brains and blood and skin. Wrapping and stretching and shaping the bones into men. Flesh? Can you see the flesh?)

Read 37:9-10

Then say, 'Breath. Can you hear the breath? Blowing and filling bodies to bursting. Breathing new life into lungs. Breath. Can you hear the breath?'

Read 37:11

Then say, 'Hope. Can you feel the hope? Hope for a new life. Hope for a new start. Hope for a home again. Hope. Can you feel the hope?'

Read 37:12-14

Then say, 'Bones and dust by God's rattling words turned to flesh and breath and hope. Hope. Can you feel the hope?'

TRINITY

Isaiah 6:1-8

Telling tips:

This reading functions like the previous one. Two readers and a series of responses intended to help the crowd reflect on what they have just heard in the reading. The scripture passages you need to read are listed between the responses, so use whichever translation you prefer.

Read 6:1

Then say, 'The Lord. Can you see the Lord? Sitting high on his throne. His robe flowing through the temple. The Lord. Can you see the Lord?'

Read 6:2-3

Then say, 'The Seraph. Can you hear the Seraph? Wings flapping. Feet and face hidden. Voices crying: "Holy, holy, holy to the Lord". Voices from beyond this world. Voices like thunder. The Seraph. Can you hear the Seraph?'

Read 6:4

Then say, 'Smoke. Can you smell the smoke? The burning of the incense. Sweet and strong and mysterious. And through the smoke, the Seraph. And their song. And the throne. And the Lord sat on high. All at once. All together. Overpowering. Overwhelming. Smoke. Can you smell the smoke?'

Read 6:5

Then say, 'Fear. Can you taste the fear? Fear mixed with sorrow. Guilt in the face of God's glory. Wonder at what will happen next. Fear. Can you taste the fear?'

Read 6:6-7

Then say, 'Coal. Can you feel the coal? Burning and cleansing. Forgiving and purifying. Lips touched and guilt gone and sin blotted out. Coal. Can you feel the coal?'

Read 6:8

Then say, 'Voice. Do you recognise the voice? God's voice and your voice combined in a chorus. Who will go? Here am I. Send me. Who will go? Here am I. Send me. Who will go? Here am I. Send me. Voice. Do you recognise the voice?'

HaRVEST

Matthew 6:25-33

Telling tips:
Tell the crowd that you will give them the actions along the way. Again, two readers, one to narrate and another to lead the crowd, might be helpful here.

Don't worry about your life. What you'll eat. What you'll drink. What you'll wear. For life is more than food. Life is more than clothing.

Look up at the birds.
Have everyone look up and flap their arms.
They don't sow. They don't reap. They don't fill up barns. But your Father in heaven feeds them. Aren't you worth more than them?

Look at your watch, or whatever you use for a timepiece.
Have everyone look at watches, phones, maybe even ask them to give you the time.
Now let me ask you, can you add even one minute to your life by worrying?

Now look at your clothes.
Have everyone look at what they are wearing.
Do lilies spin or sew or knit or crochet? No! But even Solomon in his finest gear could not compare with them. Even the loveliest lily is here today and gone tomorrow. But God clothes them. So, why not cast aside your doubts and trust that he will clothe you, too.

I'll say it again. Don't worry. About what you'll eat, or what you'll drink, or what you'll wear.
Have everyone look at their clothes again.

People who don't know God and who don't trust him do that sort of thing.
But you have a Father in heaven who knows exactly what you need.

So, seek what's important to him, live like he's called you to,

and trust him to provide the rest.

Have everyone look up and hold out their hands. Might be a good time to pray!

ALL SAINTS

Revelation 21:1-6a

Telling tips:

This takes the reflective readings a step further and asks the crowd not only to reflect on each verse, but also to share that reflection with a neighbour. Consequently, it could be noisy and take a while! The scripture passages you need to read are listed between the responses, so use whichever translation you prefer.

Read 21:1

Then say, 'A new heaven. A new earth. What might that look like? What do you imagine? Tell your neighbour what you imagine.'

Read 21:2

Then say, 'A new Jerusalem, coming down from heaven. What does that look like? What do you imagine? Tell your neighbour what you see.'

Read 21:3

Then say, 'God among us. God living with us. How would that affect things? What would life be like? Tell your neighbour what you think would happen.'

Read 21:4

Then say, 'No more tears. No more death. No more pain. What would that be like? What do you imagine? Tell your neighbour the difference that would make to you.'

Read 21:5

Then say, 'All things new. We have looked and we have imagined some of the things God will make new. Is there anything else you think he will make new, too? Tell your neighbour.'

Read 21:6a

YEAR C

ADVENT

Jeremiah 33:14-16

Telling tips:
Since this reading is so short, it might be helpful to have it projected or printed out so that folk can more easily see how the congregational words lead into what the reader says.

Have everyone say, 'The days are coming. The days are coming. The days are surely coming.'

Reader: Says the Lord, when I will make my promises come true.
My promise to Israel and to Judah.

Have everyone say, 'And in those days. And in those days. Most surely in those days.'

Reader: I will raise a righteous branch from the house of David. And that branch will bring about justice and righteousness in the land.

Have everyone say, 'Then in those days. Then in those days. Most surely in those days.'

Reader: Judah will be saved. Jerusalem will be secure. And this will be the name everyone knows it by: 'The Lord is our righteousness.'

BOB
HartMan's
AstounDing
all-age
BIBLE
ReaDinGs
for Holidays and Holy Days

CHRISTMAS EVE

Luke 2:1-14, (15-20)

Telling tips:

This is another one of those reflective readings. Use one voice for the scripture, another for the reflective response. And you might even want to add the odd Christmas carol as part of some of the responses. It would make for a nice way to journey through the reading. The scripture passages you need to read are listed between the responses, so use whichever translation you prefer.

Read 2:1-3

Then say, 'Oppression. Can you imagine the oppression? Controlled by a foreign government. Forced to pick up and move at their leader's whim. Life inconvenienced, disrupted, thrown out of kilter. Oppression. Can you feel the oppression?'

Read 2:4-5

Then say, 'Distance. Do you know the distance? Ninety miles from Nazareth to Bethlehem. Ninety long miles. And no donkey mentioned. So, all that way on your feet. Ninety miles, expecting your firstborn child. Distance. Do you know the distance?'

Read 2:6-7

Then say, 'Child. Can you see the child? Wrapped up in cloth. Asleep in the hay. Mary and Joseph near. God's only son become one of us. Child. Can you see the child?'

Read 2:8-9

Then say, 'Fear. Can you taste the fear? The dark ripped by white. A visitor bright. The sudden surprise of God's holy light. Fear? Can you taste the fear?'

Read 2:10-11

Then say, 'Hope. Can you feel the hope? A promise made real. The waiting ended. Good news, God's good news at last! Hope. Can you feel the hope?'

Read 2:12-14

Then say, 'Praise. Can you hear the praise? Angel voices. What do they sound like? Human? Or something else? Something stranger, more amazing, more beautiful? Praise. Can you hear the praise?'

Read 2:15

Then say, 'Excitement. Can you sense the excitement? Feet hammering the ground. Words buzzing round. What will he look like? What will we see? What will this Messiah be? Excitement. Can you sense the excitement?'

Read 2:16-19

Then say, 'Wonder. Can you share her wonder? The words of the shepherds. Angels, again. All coming back. All making sense. Her visitor and their visitors, too. Wonder. Can you share her wonder?'

Read 2:20

The shepherds returned, glorifying and praising God for all they had heard and seen, as it had been told them.

Then say, 'Joy! Can you shout for joy? Shout with the angels, high in the sky. And shout with the shepherds waking the town. Shout for what God has done. Joy! Can you shout for joy?'

CHRISTMAS DAY

Isaiah 9:2-7

Telling tips:
Something a little different, a poem that plays with the themes of the passage.

So, sing a song of Christmas
and raise your voice to praise
the Light who turns the darkness into day.
For unto us a child is born
and this will be his name:
Counsellor, Mighty God, Father, Prince of peace,
a king whose reign will never, ever cease.

Sing a song of Christmas
that fills the starry air
to the babe who breaks the burden we must bear.
For unto us a child is born
and this will be his name:
Counsellor, Mighty God, Father, Prince of peace,
a king whose reign will never, ever cease.

Sing a song of Christmas,
play drums and harps and flutes
to the one who burns the soldiers' trampling boots.
For unto us a child is born
and this will be his name:
Counsellor, Mighty God, Father, Prince of peace,
a king whose reign will never, ever cease.

BOB
HARTMAN'S
ASTOUNDING
ALL-AGE
BIBLE
READINGS
for Holidays and Holy Days

EPIPHANY

Psalm 72:1-7, 10-14

Telling tips:

You could print the reading out, or project it, so the congregation know where to come in. Or, you could simply teach them their line, which is less a response and more a question that sets up the description of the king and point to them when you want them to say it.

All: What kind of king do we want, O Lord? What kind of king do we need?

Reader: Give us a just king, Lord. A righteous king. Who judges your people rightly. Who treats the poor justly.

All: What kind of king do we want, O Lord? What kind of king do we need?

Reader: Let prosperity grow on the mountains, under his reign. And righteousness on the hills. Give us a king who defends the poor, delivers the needy and defeats the oppressor.

All: What kind of king do we want, O Lord? What kind of king do we need?

Reader: A king whose reign lasts as long as the sun, Lord. A king who is like the falling rain. A refreshing shower, watering the earth. A king under whom righteousness and peace will flourish and grow, grow until the moon is no more.

All: What kind of king do we want, O Lord? What kind of king do we need?

Reader: A king renowned throughout the earth, Lord. Who receives tribute from Tarshish and gifts from Sheba. A king before whom all other kings bow down.

All: What kind of king do we want, O Lord? What kind of king do we need?

Reader: A king who hears the cries of the poor, the needy, the helpless, and comes to their rescue. A king who pities the weak and is there to save them. A king who delivers them from violence and oppression. A king who cares when their blood is shed.

All: What kind of king do we want, O Lord? What kind of king do we need?

Reader: A king who sides with the weak, Lord. A kingdom for the poor.

TRANSFIGURATION

2 Corinthians 3:12 – 4:2

Telling tips:
Just two motions, here. Veiled and unveiled. For the veiled motion, have everyone put their hands in front of their faces. A crossing of the hands motion, with fingers splayed, so they can look between the gaps works very nicely. For the unveiled motion, have them make the veiled motion, then take their hands away and look ahead or up in the air.

3:12
Since, then, we have such a hope, we act with great boldness,

3:13
not like Moses, who put a veil over his face
veiled motion
to keep the people of Israel from gazing at the end of the glory
that was being set aside.

3:14
But their minds were hardened. Indeed, to this very day,
when they hear the reading of the old covenant, that same veil
veiled motion
is still there, since only in Christ is it set aside.

3:15
Indeed, to this very day whenever Moses is read, a veil
veiled motion
lies over their minds;

3:16
but when one turns to the Lord, the veil is removed.
unveiled motion

3:17
Now the Lord is the Spirit, and where the Spirit of the Lord is, there is freedom.

3:18
And all of us, with unveiled faces,

unveiled motion

seeing the glory of the Lord as though reflected in a mirror, are being
transformed into the same image from one degree of glory to another;
for this comes from the Lord, the Spirit.

4:1
Therefore, since it is by God's mercy that we are engaged in this ministry,
we do not lose heart.

4:2
We have renounced the shameful things that one hides;

veiled motion

we refuse to practise cunning or to falsify God's word; but by the open statement of the
truth we commend ourselves to the conscience of everyone in the sight of God.

unveiled motion

ASH WEDNESDAY

Isaiah 58:1-12

Telling tips:

Divide your group into two groups. Teach the first group the line, 'Why do we fast, but you do not see? Why humble ourselves, but you do not notice?' And teach the second group the other response, 'Then what if we choose the fast you choose?' Then simply point to the group you want the response from. Or, you could print out or project their responses along with the rest of the text. The scripture passages you need to read are listed between the responses, so use whichever translation you prefer.

Read 58:1-2

Have everyone say, 'Why do we fast, but you do not see?
Why humble ourselves, but you do not notice?'

Read 58:3b

Have everyone say, 'Why do we fast, but you do not see?
Why humble ourselves, but you do not notice?'

Read 58:4

Have everyone say, 'Why do we fast, but you do not see?
Why humble ourselves, but you do not notice?'

Read 58:5

Have everyone say, 'Why do we fast, but you do not see?
Why humble ourselves, but you do not notice?'

Read 58:6-7

Have everyone say, 'Then what if we choose the fast you choose?'

Read 58:8

Have everyone say, 'Then what if we choose the fast you choose?'

Read 58:9-10

Have everyone say, 'Then what if we choose the fast you choose?

Read 58:11-12

PALM SUNDAY

Luke 19:28-40

Telling tips:

Divide your group into four sections. One for the owner of the colt.
One for the disciples. One for the crowd of disciples. One for the Pharisees.
Teach them their (very simple) lines, ahead of time. You might also want
to project them, as well, or lead them in those lines when the time comes.
You will narrate and do Jesus' lines.

Owner line (spoken in a slightly disgruntled fashion):
'Why are you untying my colt?'

Disciple line (spoken matter-of-factly, with a shrug):
'The Lord needs it.'

Crowd line (spoken exuberantly):
'Blessed is the king who comes in the name of the Lord!'

Pharisee line (spoken in a worried fashion):
'Stop your disciples, teacher!'

After Jesus said this, he went ahead, towards Jerusalem. When he drew near to
Bethphage and Bethany, at the Mount of Olives, he said to two of his disciples,
"In the next village, just as you enter, you will find a colt that has never been ridden.
Untie the colt and bring it to me. If anyone asks you:

Owner group

'Why are you untying my colt?', you must answer:

Disciple group

'The Lord needs it.'"

So, the disciples went into the village and found the colt, just as Jesus had said.
But when they went to untie it, the owner said:

Owner group

'Why are you untying my colt?' And the disciples answered:

Disciple group

'The Lord needs it.'

When they took the colt to Jesus, they put their cloaks on its back and then set Jesus on it. He rode along on the colt and people laid their cloaks on the road in front of him.

They started down the path that led from the Mount of Olives into Jerusalem. And as they went, a huge crowd of Jesus' disciples praised God, joyfully, shouting out their amazement at all the powerful things they had seen Jesus do:

Crowd group
'Blessed is the king who comes in the name of the Lord!'

But some of the Pharisees who were in the crowd said to Jesus:

Pharisee group
'Stop your disciples, teacher!'

'If my disciples fell silent,' Jesus replied, 'the stones themselves would shout out!'

GOOD FRIDAY

Psalm 22

Telling tips:

Another reflective response reading, although this one, much like the Psalm itself, is addressed to God. Two readers, one for the passage and the other for the reflection, would work best here, I think. The scripture passages you need to read are listed between the responses, so use whichever translation you prefer.

Read 22:1-2

Then say, 'Groaning. Can you hear me groaning, Lord? I'm here. I'm in pain. I'm crying out to you. Crying for your help. So, why aren't you listening? Why don't you answer? Groaning. Can you hear me groaning, Lord?'

Read 22:3-5

Then say, 'Memories. I have memories, Lord. Memories of the way you helped your people in the past. Seas parted. Giants defeated. Promises kept. More than kept. They trusted you. And you were there for them. Memories. I have memories, Lord.'

Read 22:6-8

Then say, 'Worm. Am I a worm, Lord? That's what they tell me. And that's how I feel. They despise me. They mock me. And when they tell me to trust in you, their words are filled with sarcasm. Worm. Am I a worm, Lord?'

Read 22:9-10

Then say, 'Memories. More memories, Lord. My own memories. The others cannot be right, Lord. I am not a worm. For I remember. From the moment I was born, you were there for me. And from that moment you have been my God. Memories. Memories of you, Lord.'

Read 22:11-18

Then say, 'Surrounded. I am surrounded, Lord. Raging bulls. Roaring lions. Packs of dogs. And I am melted, broken, dried up, shrivelled, desiccated, robbed and naked, choking on the dust of death.'

Read 22:19-21

Then say, 'So save me. Save me, Lord. From sword and tooth and claw and horn. Come quickly. Come and help me! And when you do . . .'

Read 22:22-31

Then say, 'Praise. I will praise you, Lord. Along with everyone you deliver. The poor and the afflicted. And nations will see and people will know – even people yet to be born – that you have done it. That you can do it. That you are Lord. That you are King. That you listen when we cry. That you answer.'

EaSTER DaY

1 Corinthians 15:19-26

Telling tips:

Divide your group into two groups. One to represent death and dying, the other to represent resurrection.

The death group will cover their heads or faces with their hands, frown and look down.

The resurrection group will raise their hands slowly into the air, smile and look up.

If our hope in Christ is for this life only, then we should be pitied. Pitied above everyone.
Death group motion

But the reality is that Christ has, indeed, been raised from the dead.
Resurrection group motion

He is the beginning of the harvest, the first fruit to be picked and gathered in,
of all the dead who will rise after him.
Death came through a human being.
Death group motion

So, the resurrection also comes through a human being.
Resurrection group motion

All died in Adam.
Death group motion

So, all will be made alive through Christ.
Resurrection group motion

And here is the order:

Christ raised first, like the first barley or wheat or apples of a glorious harvest.

Resurrection group motion

And then, when he comes, the ones who belong to him.

Resurrection group motion

Then the end will come. And that is when he will pass the kingdom onto God, the Father, after he has destroyed every evil power. He must reign, you see, until every enemy submits to him.

And the last enemy to be destroyed? Death itself.

Death group motion

It might then be nice to have both groups finish with the resurrection motion, to signify the end of death.

ASCENSION

Acts 1:1-11

Telling tips:

It could be helpful to have one person lead the crowd in their words and actions and another to read the passage. It could also work with everyone's lines projected or written out. The scripture passages you need to read are listed between the responses, so use whichever translation you prefer.

Have everyone pretend to leaf through the pages of a book and say,
'First, a few words about the prequel.'

Read 1:1-2

Have everyone pretend to roll a stone away and say,
'And now, a word or two about the resurrection.'

Read 1:3

Have everyone make a 'stay' motion and say,
'Which includes one simple instruction and one amazing promise.'

Read 1:4-5

Have everyone put a hand in the air, as if asking a question and say,
'Next, there is a rather important question.'

Read 1:6

Have everyone shrug their shoulders and say,
'And a reasonably vague answer.'

Read 1:7

Have everyone make a muscle and say,

'Followed by another promise and another instruction.

Read 1:8

Have everyone look up and say,

'And finally, the ascension!'

Read 1:9-11

PENTECOST

Romans 8:14-17

His Spirit leads me, this I know,
I am a child of God;
his Spirit shows me where to go,
I am a child of God.
Set free from fear, I'm not a slave,
I am adopted, I am saved;
I am a child of God,
I am a child of God.

For when the words fly from my lips,
crying Abba Father,
the Spirit says that I am his,
crying Abba Father,
and when the words fly from my lips,
crying Abba Father,
that's what his Spirit witnesses,
crying Abba Father.

And therefore I'm my father's heir,
I am a child of God;
joint heirs with brother Jesus,
I am a child of God.
To suffer with him is my story,
together with him in his glory,
I am a child of God,
I am a child of God.

BOB
Hartman's
Astounding
All-Age
Bible
Readings
for Holidays and Holy Days

TRINITY

John 16:12-15

Telling tips:
Lead the congregation in the actions as you reach them in the text.
Again, you could use a second person to lead the actions.

'There are so many things I still need to tell you, but you won't be able to bear them, now.

But the Spirit of truth will come to you. And when he does, he will:

Lead you to all the truth.
Have everyone point forward, as if pointing the way to something.

He won't be speaking on his own.
Everyone put a hand to the side of their mouth, as if calling out or announcing something.

No, he will tell you what he hears.
Everybody put a hand to their ear, as if listening to something.

And he will make plain to you what is to come.
Everybody put a hand over their eyes, as if peering into the future.

It's me he will glorify.
Everyone hold one hand in the air.

For he will take what's mine and make it plain to you.
With that hand in the air, have everyone pretend to grasp something, then pass it on to their neighbour.

All that belongs to the Father belongs to me.
That's why I say he will take what's mine and make it plain to you.'
Repeat previous action.

HARVEST

Psalm 100

Telling tips:
This reading is meant to be big and noisy. Do it with everyone standing up.

100:1: Make a joyful noise to the LORD, all the earth.

Reader: Make a noise, a noise of joy.

All: Make it to the Lord, O earth!
Have everyone give a joyful shout here.

Reader: Worship him gladly.

All: Sing when you come into his presence.
Have everyone sing a big Aaaaaa!

Reader: Our Lord is God. We know it!

All: He made us. We belong to him. We're his people. We're his sheep.
Have everyone make a big joyful BAAAAA here, maybe even a sung version like the previous Aaaaaa!

Reader: Give thanks when you pass through his gates.

All: And when you are in his courts, give him praise.
Have everyone shout or sing — a combination of the above, maybe.

Reader: I'll say it again, give him thanks.

All: And bless his name.
Have everyone shout, 'We bless you, Lord!'

Reader: For our Lord is good! His loving faithfulness never ends.

All: And it extends to every generation.
One more big shout of praise.

ALL SAINTS

Luke 6:20-31

Telling tips:

Divide your group into two groups. One for the poor and one for the rich. Then teach them their responses. The poor say 'Huh?' in a confused manner after the first part of each blessing, and then 'Oh!' in a delighted fashion after the second part. The rich also say 'Huh?' in a confused fashion after the first part of each woe, and then say 'Oh, dear!' in a woeful manner, after the second part.

So, Jesus looked at his disciples and said:

Those of you who are poor are blessed,
Poor group 'Huh?'
for the kingdom of God belongs to you.
Poor group 'Oh!'

And if you're hungry, if your tummy is rumbling even now,
you are blessed, too,
Poor group 'Huh?'
for that tummy will be filled.
Poor group 'Oh!'

And if you're weeping, you too are blessed,
Poor group 'Huh?'
for you will break out in laughter.
Poor group 'Oh!'

You are blessed when people hate you, too.
Poor group 'Huh?'
And when they kick you out of their group.
Poor group 'Huh?'

And when they say nasty things about you.

Poor group 'Huh?'

And when they tell lies about you, too, because you follow me.

Poor group 'Huh?'

Be glad when that happens and jump for joy

Poor group 'Huh?'

because you will surely be rewarded in heaven,

Poor group 'Oh!'

for that is exactly how their ancestors treated the prophets.

But if you're rich, you're gonna be sorry

Rich group 'Huh?'

because you have already received every good thing you're gonna get.

Rich group 'Oh, dear!'

And if your belly is full now, you're gonna be sorry

Rich group 'Huh?'

because you're going to find out what it means to be hungry.

Rich group 'Oh, dear!'

And, yeah, if you're laughing now, you're gonna be sorry

Rich group 'Huh?'

because you're going to mourn and weep.

Rich group 'Oh, dear!'

And when people praise you and say good things about you, you're gonna be sorry

Rich group 'Huh?'

because that's what the people who came before them said about the false prophets.

Rich group 'Oh, dear!'

So, listen up. Here's what I have to say:

Love your enemies.

Everybody 'Huh?'

Do good things for people who hate you.

Everybody 'Huh?'

Give your blessing to the person who curses you.

Everybody 'Huh?'

Lift up your prayers for those who abuse you.

Everybody 'Huh?'

If somebody hits you on one cheek, offer him the other one.

Everybody 'Huh?'

And if someone takes your coat, give him your shirt as well.

Everybody 'Huh?'

Give to every beggar.

Everybody 'Huh?'

And let the thief keep what he steals from you.

Everybody 'Huh?'

Treat other people the same way you would have them treat you.

Everybody 'Oh!'